dolcissimo

dolcissimo

delicious sweet things from Italy

Maxine Clark Photography by Jean Cazals

RYLAND
PETERS
& SMALL

LONDON NEW YORK

Published in the United States in 2004
by Ryland Peters & Small, Inc.
519 Broadway, 5th Floor,
New York, NY 1001
www.rylandpeters.com

10 9 8 7 6 5 4 3 2 1

Library of Congress Cataloging-in-
Publication Data

Clark, Maxine.
  Dolcissimo : delicious sweet things from
Italy / Maxine Clark ;
photography by Jean Cazals.
      p. cm.
Includes index.
  ISBN 1-84172-582-X
  1. Confectionery. 2. Cookery, Italian.
I. Title.
  TX783.C58 2004
  641.8'6'0945--dc21
                2003012746

Senior Designer Steve Painter
Commissioning Editor
Elsa Petersen-Schepelern
Editor Susan Stuck
Production Deborah Wehner
Art Director Gabriella Le Grazie
Publishing Director Alison Starling

Food Stylist Maxine Clark
Assistant Food Stylists
Kate Habershon
Laura Lennox-Conyngham
Stylist Helen Trent

Author's acknowledgments
Special thanks go to Kate and Laura,
for both nursing and recipe testing.
Thank you to Jean, for his enthusiasm
and professionalism, to Steve for his
patience, calmness, and coffees at the
studio (and also a lovely looking book),
and to the ever-patient Elsa, my editor,
for her undying enthusiasm, support, and
her fabulous ice cream machine!

Publishers' acknowledgments
All photographs are by Jean Cazals with
the exception of page 27, by Debi Treloar.

Notes
• All spoon measurements are level
unless otherwise specified.
• All eggs are large unless otherwise
specified. Uncooked or partly cooked
eggs should not be served to the very
young, the very old, those with
compromised immune systems, or
to pregnant women.
• Before baking, weigh or measure all
ingredients exactly and prepare baking
pans or sheets.
• Ovens should be preheated to the
specified temperature. Recipes in this
book were tested in several kinds of
oven—all work slightly differently.
I recommend using an oven thermometer
and consulting the maker's handbook for
special instructions.

contents

dolce, dolci, dolcissimo!

Italians have the world's sweetest tooth. No excuse is needed to partake of dolci, be it ice cream, chocolate, a cake, or a confection packed with fruit and nuts.

The variety of dolci (literally "sweets") and desserts in Italy is incredible, and because local pastry stores make the best dolci, few people make them at home. Just walk past a window display of a speciality *pasticceria* anywhere in Italy and your eyes will pop out on stalks. I particularly remember one in Assisi—it had piles of huge meringues, like clouds hovering on silver trays. They were so enormous I wondered if there were a special technique for eating them. There was a vast array of cakes studded with dried fruits, candied fruits and nuts, piles of little biscotti crunchy with almonds and pine nuts, large open tarts filled with brightly colored preserves, and neatly stacked bars of sticky torrone. Crossing the threshold was no problem, but choosing what to sample was almost impossible—especially when I saw the gelato counter with nearly 30 different flavors, soft and smooth and just waiting to be plopped into a tub or smeared onto a crisp cone.

Throughout history, Italian pastry chefs have taken the art of dolci-making wherever they went in the world—France, America, even Britain, where Italian ice cream has become a national treasure. These masters of their art were employed originally by royalty and the nobility. The ingredients they used were the most expensive in their day—preserved fruit and nuts, honey, sugar, and spices. Gradually, over the centuries, pastry chefs would set up their own businesses to reach the masses, but buying a

dolce today still retains a certain feeling of occasion in Italy. Dolci of all kinds are taken as gifts to friends and family, while incredible, complicated, artistic confections are ordered for special occasions such as christenings and weddings. For these events, dolci are served with a glass of spumante or prosecco—for less splendid occasions, good Italian coffee or a delicious sweet wine are the preferred companions.

Italy is blessed with a geography and climate that will grow virtually anything. To the north, there is plenty of butter and cream and sweet chestnuts to make desserts like Monte Bianco. In central Italy, fruits abound to be made into open tarts and preserves. In the south, people could not live a day without a gelato or granita, and something with almonds in it. Almonds, sugar, and candied fruit were brought to Sicily during the Moorish conquest, and infiltrated the repertoire of Italian dolci. Many delectable dolci made from almonds are still handmade by nuns in Sicily, to supplement their income.

Spices like cinnamon, cloves, black pepper, coriander, and allspice arrived during the Renaissance from the East via Venice and subtly enhance all sorts of rich, sticky confections, still made in the same, time-honored way as in the medieval era—think of *panforte di Siena*.

But Italian dolci are always evolving—take the ubiquitous tiramisù, for example, said to have originated in Venice in the 1950s, now a worldwide favorite. This book contains a distillation of the multitude of dolci to be found in Italy, hence the name *Dolcissimo*. Simply the best sweet things in the world.

fruit desserts

Strawberries with balsamic may sound strange, but this resinous syrup brings out their sweetness. Try a strawberry sorbet laced with a tablespoon of balsamic: undetectable, but even the least flavorsome fruits taste better.

strawberries with balsamic syrup and mascarpone ice cream

fragole allo sciroppo balsamico con gelato di mascarpone

1½ lb. ripe strawberries, halved

mascarpone ice cream

2¼ cups whole milk

1 vanilla bean

5 large egg yolks

½ cup plus 2 tablespoons sugar

1½ cups heavy cream

1¼ cups mascarpone cheese

balsamic syrup

1 cup sugar

2 tablespoons balsamic vinegar

an ice cream maker

serves 4
makes 1 quart ice cream

To make the ice cream, put the milk in a saucepan. Split the vanilla bean lengthwise, scrape out the seeds and add the bean and seeds to the milk. Heat until almost boiling, remove from the heat, stir well, and set aside to infuse for 30 minutes.

Put the egg yolks and sugar in a bowl and beat until pale and creamy. Add the milk and vanilla bean and mix well. Return the mixture to the pan and remove the vanilla bean (which can be rinsed, dried, and used to flavor a jar of sugar). Cook the mixture over low heat, stirring constantly, until it is thick enough to coat the back of a wooden spoon. It must not boil or it will separate. Remove from the heat and stir in the cream. Let cool completely.

When cold, use a hand-held electric beater to beat the custard into the mascarpone. Chill, then freeze in an ice cream maker, transfer to a freezer container, and store in the freezer.

To make the balsamic syrup, put the sugar, balsamic vinegar, and 1 cup water in a small saucepan. Heat gently until the sugar dissolves. Bring to a boil and boil rapidly for 5 minutes until reduced by one-quarter. Remove from the heat, cool, then chill.

Toss the strawberries in the syrup. Transfer the ice cream to the refrigerator at least 20 minutes before serving, to soften. Serve the strawberries with scoops of mascarpone ice cream, then trail any remaining syrup over the top.

The dessert equivalent of a Bellini—and much more enjoyable to linger over on a hot summer's night. Peaches and chilled prosecco, a sparkling wine from the Veneto, are a perfect marriage. The object is to spoon out the fruit and sup the flavored wine while engaged in scintillating conversation. This my favorite way to eat fresh, golden peaches kissed by the sun.

peaches and raspberries in sparkling wine

pesche e lamponi con prosecco

4 perfect ripe peaches

¼ cup sugar

¼ cup raspberry liqueur (framboise)

½ cup fresh raspberries, plus extra to serve

1 bottle chilled prosecco wine (750 ml)

serves 4

Skin and slice the peaches into a bowl, mix with the sugar, liqueur, and raspberries. Cover and chill for at least 1 hour.

When ready to serve, spoon the macerated peaches into 4 large glasses. Top up with prosecco at the table, add some extra raspberries, and serve with long spoons.

There is nothing quite as sensual as warm zabaglione served straight from the pan. Many like to cook it in a copper bowl so that it cooks quickly. The secret is not to let the mixture get too hot, though still hot enough to cook and thicken the egg yolks. The proportions are easy to remember; one tablespoon sugar, to one egg yolk, to one tablespoon Marsala will serve one person. It must be made at the last moment, but it doesn't take long.

warm zabaglione with pears poached in marsala

zabaglione con pere cotte al marsala

1⅓ cups sweet white wine

1⅓ cups Marsala wine

1 cup sugar

1 vanilla bean, split, seeds scraped out and reserved

6 firm but ripe pears

1 teaspoon vanilla extract

zabaglione

6 large egg yolks

6 tablespoons Marsala wine

6 tablespoons sugar

to serve (optional)

chopped pan-toasted hazelnuts

mint leaves

serves 6

To poach the pears, put the white wine, Marsala, sugar, and the split vanilla bean and seeds in a saucepan and bring to a boil. Peel the fruit carefully, but leave their stalks on, and shave a thin slice from the base so they will stand up. Stand the pears in the wine in the saucepan—they should just fit. Spoon over a little liquid to prevent discoloration. Cover tightly and simmer for about 25 minutes, turning occasionally, until tender. Let cool in the liquid.

Remove the vanilla bean. Lift out the pears and set in a serving dish. Boil the liquid until reduced to 1¼ cups. Stir in the vanilla extract. Cool, then pour over the pears. Chill until ready to serve.

Make the zabaglione at the last minute. Put the egg yolks, Marsala, and sugar in a medium heatproof bowl and beat with a hand-held electric mixer or a whisk until well blended. Set over a saucepan of gently simmering water—the base should at no time be in contact with the water. Do not let the water boil. Beat the mixture until it is glossy, pale, light, fluffy, and holds a trail when dropped from the beaters. This should take about 5 minutes. To serve, spoon a pool of syrup onto a plate, add 1–2 spoonfuls of zabaglione, then stand a pear on top. Sprinkle with nuts and mint, if using.

A semifreddo is a dessert that is half frozen to give it a slightly thickened, creamy texture. Sometimes it is made of whipped cream lightened with meringue, then flavoured with anything from vanilla to passionfruit. In this example, the espresso gives an interesting texture, but you must buy it very finely ground.

coffee semifreddo with espresso
semifreddo affogato al caffè

1½ cups ricotta cheese, at room temperature

1½ cups mascarpone cheese, at room temperature

1 tablespoon dark rum

3 tablespoons Tia Maria, Kahlua, or other coffee liqueur

1 teaspoon vanilla extract

¼ cup confectioners' sugar, or to taste

2 tablespoons finely ground espresso Italian roast coffee

to serve

softly whipped cream

6–8 tiny cups of hot espresso coffee

bittersweet chocolate wafers

6–8 flexible ice cream molds or small ramekins

serves 6–8

Put the ricotta and mascarpone in a bowl, and beat with a wooden spoon. (Do not attempt to do this in a food processor or the mixture will be too runny.) Beat in the rum, Tia Maria, vanilla extract, and confectioners' sugar. Fold in the ground espresso so that the mixture is marbled. Carefully spoon into the ice cream molds or ramekins, piling the mixture high. Freeze for 2 hours.

Transfer to the refrigerator 15–20 minutes before serving to soften slightly. The mixture should be only just frozen or very chilled. Just before serving, dip the molds quickly in warm water and invert into chilled shallow bowls. Serve immediately with tiny cups of espresso for guests to pour over the semifreddo.

mint sorbet

sorbetto alla menta

Italians are very fond of sweet and sticky liqueurs, so I have laced this sorbetto with crème de menthe—bliss.

1½ cups sugar

2 cups dry white wine, such as sauvignon blanc, chilled

1½ cups fresh mint leaves

2 tablespoons fresh lime juice

2–3 tablespoons crème de menthe liqueur

an ice cream maker

makes about 1 quart

Put the sugar and 2 cups water in a saucepan and bring slowly to a boil, stirring until the sugar dissolves. Remove from the heat, then stir in the wine and 1 cup of the mint leaves. Let cool, then chill for several hours. Strain the syrup into a blender. Add the remaining mint leaves, lime juice, and liqueur. Blend until the leaves disappear and the syrup is speckled green.

Pour into an ice cream maker and freeze according to the manufacturer's instructions. Transfer to a chilled freezer container, cover, and freeze until firm. Let soften in the refrigerator for 20 minutes before serving.

cantaloupe melon ice cream

gelato di melone

1 small, very ripe, orange-fleshed cantaloupe or charentais melon, about 2½ lb., halved and seeded

⅔ cup sugar

3 tablespoons light corn syrup

1 tablespoon freshly squeezed lemon juice

3 cups whole milk

⅔ cup skimmed milk powder

1 teaspoon powdered gelatin

an ice cream maker

serves 8

Scoop out the melon flesh into a food processor or blender. Add the sugar, syrup, and lemon juice and purée until smooth.

Pour the milk into a saucepan and beat in the dried milk powder and gelatin. Bring slowly to just below the boil. Stir in the melon purée and transfer to a bowl to cool. When cold, chill in the refrigerator for at least 1 hour or overnight.

When thoroughly chilled, transfer to an ice cream maker and freeze according to the manufacturer's instructions. Transfer to a chilled freezer container, cover, and freeze until firm. Let soften in the refrigerator for 20 minutes before serving.

A beautiful pink, exotic sorbetto from Sicily, delicately perfumed with a hint of cinnamon or jasmine flower water. Just for fun, the chocolate chips represent the black watermelon seeds, but they do add a nice crunchy texture. You won't need a whole watermelon for this recipe, so keep the rest to eat on its own.

watermelon sorbetto with chocolate chip seeds

sorbetto di anguria

1½ lb. red watermelon flesh, cut into cubes, about 4 cups

¾ cup sugar (or a bit less if the melon is very sweet)

1 small cinnamon stick

freshly squeezed juice of 2 ripe lemons

a little pink food coloring, if necessary

⅓ cup chocolate chips

an ice cream maker*

serves 4–6

*Freeze in an ice cream maker for the best results.

Remove the seeds from the melon with the tip of a small knife. Put the flesh in a food processor and purée until smooth. With the machine running, pour in the sugar and blend for 30 seconds.

Pour the melon mixture into a saucepan and add the cinnamon stick. Slowly bring to a boil, stirring all the time to dissolve the sugar completely, then turn down the heat to a bare simmer for 1 minute. Remove from the heat, then add the lemon juice, and a few drops of pink food coloring if necessary.

Let cool. When cold, remove the cinnamon stick and chill the mixture in the refrigerator for at least 1 hour (or overnight—this makes freezing quicker).

Transfer to an ice cream maker and freeze according to the manufacturer's instructions. Stir in the chocolate chips when the sorbetto is still soft. Transfer to a chilled freezer container, cover, and freeze until firm. Let soften in the refrigerator for 20 minutes before serving.

Alternatively, pour into a shallow freezer tray and freeze until the sorbetto is frozen around the edges. Mash well with a fork. When it is half frozen again, blend in a food processor until creamy, stir in the chocolate chips, then cover and freeze until firm. Let soften in the refrigerator for 20 minutes before serving.

I first tasted this on a searingly hot day in Siracusa, looking out over a peacock sea—it was sublime and just the thing to soothe a parched throat. It is very delicate, with ice crystals melting on the tongue. Orange flower water is sometimes used to perfume this granita, but I like the extra almond flavor the liqueur gives.

almond milk granita, laced with amaretto

granita di mandorle e amaretto

⅔ cup blanched almonds

½ cup sugar

1 quart ice water

3 tablespoons Amaretto liqueur

a shallow freezer tray, about 1 inch deep

serves 8

Put the almonds and sugar in a food processor and grind as finely as you can. Add 2 cups ice water and process for 2–3 minutes until very milky.

Pour this mixture into a blender with the remaining 2 cups water (you may have to do this in 2 batches). Blend on high speed for 2–3 minutes to grind the almonds as finely as possible. Pour into a bowl or pitcher, cover, and transfer to the refrigerator for several hours or overnight for the almonds to settle. Strain the settled almond milk from the sediment through a fine sieve or cheesecloth into the freezer tray. Stir in the Amaretto.

Cover and freeze for about 30 minutes, until the edges start to freeze. Scrape the frozen edges into the center with a fork and mash the mixture evenly. Repeat every 30 minutes until it forms a mound of shimmering ice crystals. Serve in chilled glasses with your prettiest silver spoons.

Tip For fresher-tasting almonds, it is better to blanch your own. Pour boiling water over whole almonds with their skins on. Leave for 2–3 minutes, then lift out a spoonful and pop them out of their skins. Continue until all are peeled.

Panna cotta is a silky smooth, set cream, originating from the Piedmont region of Italy. My version is a bit firmer as it is made with mascarpone, a rich cream cheese, and has a golden cap of caramel.

caramelized panna cotta

panna cotta caramellata

⅔ cup mascarpone cheese

2 cups heavy cream

finely pared zest of
1 unwaxed orange

½ cup plus 2 tablespoons sugar

1 vanilla bean, split lengthwise

¼ cup whole milk

2 teaspoons powdered gelatin

caramel

⅓ cup sugar

safflower oil, for oiling the molds

*6 molds, ½ cup each,
lightly oiled*

a baking tray

serves 6

To make the caramel, put the sugar and 2 tablespoons water in a heavy saucepan over low heat. Heat until the sugar dissolves, then boil to a golden caramel. Quickly pour the caramel into the oiled molds to coat evenly. Let set. Put the mascarpone, cream, orange zest, sugar, and vanilla bean in a saucepan. Set over low heat until almost but not quite boiling, stirring occasionally. Remove from the heat and leave to infuse for 20 minutes.

Put the milk into another saucepan and sprinkle the gelatin over the top. Set over very low heat until the gelatin dissolves. Stir the dissolved gelatin into the hot cream and mascarpone mixture and strain into a pitcher. Pour into the caramel-lined moulds, let cool, then refrigerate for several hours or overnight until set.

To serve, carefully loosen the creams and turn out onto individual plates. Serve at once.

Note If mascarpone is unobtainable, use heavy cream instead. The result will be less rich, but still delicious.

The sweetened vanilla and chestnut purée used in this classic chestnut dessert is usually piled high in a mound to resemble the mountain on the French-Italian border. It does look spectacular, but I like to pipe the purée into coils in glass cappuccino cups—so much easier to serve. Sometimes, I hide a meringue underneath. Dried chestnuts are available all year round from Italian gourmet stores and natural food stores, although fresh ones taste better.

monte bianco

1 lb. fresh chestnuts or
8 oz. Italian dried chestnuts

a large pinch of salt

1½ cups whole milk

½ cup plus 2 tablespoons sugar

2 tablespoons unsalted butter

2 tablespoons Cognac or grappa

2 teaspoons real vanilla extract

6 small meringues

1¼ cups heavy cream

3 tablespoons confectioners' sugar

to serve

chocolate shavings

confectioners' sugar

unsweetened cocoa powder

a pastry bag with a thin tip

serves 4–6

If using dried chestnuts, put them in a large saucepan, cover with water, and let soak overnight. The next day, change the water and add the salt. Bring to a boil and simmer for 30 minutes. Drain and return to the saucepan with the milk, sugar, and butter.

If using fresh chestnuts, slit each one down the rounded side. Put the chestnuts in a saucepan, add the salt, and cover with water. Bring to a boil and simmer for 20 minutes—by this time you should be able to peel off the shells and skins while they are still warm—if not, cook a little longer.

Put the chestnuts in a saucepan with the milk, sugar, and butter. Heat to simmering and simmer for at least 20 minutes until completely tender and even disintegrating, and the liquid has been reduced by two-thirds. Transfer to a food processor, add the Cognac and vanilla, and purée until smooth. Let cool, then spoon into a pastry bag fitted with a thin tip.

Put a meringue in the base of each cup and pipe squiggles of chestnut purée all over to hide it and form a "mountain." Put the cream and confectioners' sugar in a bowl and whip until soft peaks form. Spoon a snowy cap of cream onto each mound, sprinkle with shards of chocolate, and dust with confectioners' sugar and cocoa powder—serve immediately.

Amazingly popular, tiramisù is said to have originated in Venice in the 1950s. For added texture, I like to pulverize real chocolate in a blender for layering and sprinkling. Some recipes are too sweet for my taste, but you can add more sugar to the cream mixture if you like. Make in a large glass dish or in small glasses for a special occasion.

tiramisù

2 egg yolks

6 tablespoons Marsala wine

⅓ cup sugar

6 oz. bittersweet chocolate

1 cup mascarpone cheese

2 tablespoons dark rum

1¼ cups heavy cream

½ cup Italian espresso coffee

24 savoiardi cookies (store-bought or homemade—recipe page 41)

serves 4–6

To make the zabaglione, put the egg yolks, 2 tablespoons of the Marsala, and 2 tablespoons of the sugar in a medium heatproof bowl and beat with a hand-held electric mixer or a whisk until well blended. Set over a saucepan of gently simmering water (the bottom should at no time be in contact with the water). Do not let the water boil.

Beat the mixture until it is glossy, pale, light, and fluffy and holds a trail when dropped from the beaters, about 5 minutes. Remove from the heat and beat until cold.

Put the chocolate in a blender or food processor and grind to a powder. Set aside. Put the mascarpone and remaining sugar in a bowl and beat well, then beat in another 2 tablespoons Marsala and the rum. Gently fold into the zabaglione.

Beat the cream until soft peaks form, then fold into the zabaglione mixture. Mix the espresso and remaining Marsala in a bowl. Dip the savoiardi into the espresso mixture one at a time—don't leave them in for too long or they will disintegrate. Start assembling the tiramisù by setting half the dipped fingers in the bottom of a serving dish or 4–6 glasses. Sprinkle with any leftover coffee. Sprinkle with one-third of the pulverized chocolate. Spoon over half the mascarpone mixture, arrange the remaining savoiardi on top, moisten with any remaining coffee, and sprinkle with half the remaining chocolate. Finally spoon over the remaining mascarpone mixture and finish with a thick layer of chocolate. Chill in the refrigerator for at last 3 hours (overnight is better) for the flavors to develop. Serve chilled.

5 eggs, separated

1 cup plus 2 tablespoons sugar

1 teaspoon vanilla extract

1 teaspoon rum or Marsala wine

1⅓ cups all-purpose flour

cassata filling

2 cups fresh ricotta cheese

¼ cup heavy cream

2 eggs, separated

½ cup plus 2 tablespoons sugar

½ cup chopped mixed candied peel

2 tablespoons coarsely chopped multicolored candied cherries

⅓ cup shelled pistachios, coarsely chopped

2 oz. bittersweet chocolate, coarsely chopped

½ teaspoon ground cinnamon

finely grated zest and juice of 1 small unwaxed orange

2 tablespoons orange flower water

to serve

4–6 tablespoons hot water

5 cups confectioners' sugar, sifted

green food coloring

2–3 tablespoons chopped pistachios, or fresh jasmine flowers and leaves (optional)

a 9-inch cake pan, buttered, floured, and lined with parchment paper

an 8-inch springform cake pan

serves 8–10

Another kind of semifreddo, this glorious concoction makes a wonderful centerpiece for a summer party and contains all the essential sweet flavors of Sicily. The mixture will look very runny when it is poured into the lined pan—don't worry; it will thicken as it freezes.

cassata siciliana

Start the day before you want to serve. To make the cake, put the egg yolks, sugar, vanilla, and rum in a bowl and beat until pale and mousse-like (an electric food mixer gives the best results). Sift the flour onto a sheet of wax paper. Beat the egg whites until stiff, then gently fold into the egg and sugar mixture. Gradually fold in the flour. Pour into the prepared 9-inch cake pan and bake in a preheated oven at 350°F for 30–35 minutes until golden, firm, and well risen. Invert onto a wire rack to cool completely.

When cold, peel off the paper, cut the cake into thin slices, and use them to line the base and sides of the cassata pan, reserving enough slices to cover the top.

To make the cassata filling, press the ricotta through a sieve into a bowl and work in the cream, egg yolks, and sugar. Stir in the peel, cherries, pistachios, chocolate, cinnamon, orange juice, grated zest, and orange flower water. Beat the egg whites stiffly and fold into the mixture. Spoon the mixture into the sponge-lined 8-inch pan and cover with the remaining sponge. Chill or freeze until just firm.

To finish the cassata, slip a knife around the sides to loosen it and invert it onto a pretty plate. Put the hot water and confectioners' sugar in a bowl and beat with a wooden spoon until smooth and only just pourable. Tint with food coloring to the palest pistachio green. Pour over the center of the cassata and let the frosting flow over the sides to cover. It needs no further embellishment except a sprinkle of chopped pistachio nuts or a few jasmine flowers, plus jasmine leaves around the edge, if available. To serve, cut in wedges like a cake.

tarts

1 recipe Pasta Frolla dough
(page 63)

marmellata di zucca

1 lb. dense orange-fleshed
pumpkin, halved, seeded, peeled,
and cut into 1½-inch chunks

¾ cup sugar

2 large eggs, beaten

¼ teaspoon dry English
mustard powder

¼ teaspoon ground cinnamon

grated zest and juice of
1 unwaxed lemon or orange

6 tablespoons unsalted
butter, melted

¼ cup chopped candied melon or
orange peel (optional)

sugar, for dusting

a tart pan or pie plate,
9 inches diameter, 2 inches deep

serves 6–8
makes one 9-inch deep tart

Jam tarts are very popular throughout Italy, but this is the best and most unusual I have tasted. Adding the mustard powder gives the pumpkin a bit of a bite. Maybe this updated Renaissance recipe is the precursor to American pumpkin pie. Italians love candied fruit, but if you prefer a smoother result, omit it or sprinkle it on top after baking.

spiced pumpkin curd tart

crostata alla marmellata di zucca

Cut one-third off the ball of dough and reserve to make a lattice. Put the remaining two-thirds on a floured surface, roll out to about ¼ inch thick, and use to line the tart pan or pie plate. Trim and chill or freeze for 15 minutes.

To make the *marmellata*, steam the pumpkin for about 40 minutes, until it is tender. Drain and let cool. Put the pumpkin in a blender or food processor with the sugar, eggs, mustard powder, cinnamon, lemon zest, juice, and melted butter, then purée until smooth. Strain through a sieve into a heatproof bowl set over a saucepan of barely simmering water. Cook gently, stirring often at the beginning, then continuously at the end until the mixture coats the back of a spoon, about 30 minutes. Do not let the mixture boil or it will curdle. Fold in the candied fruit, if using. Let cool to room temperature.

Pour the filling into the tart crust and level the surface. Roll out the remaining dough and cut into narrow strips. Use these strips to make a lattice on top of the tart—you can be as creative as you like. Brush the dough with a little water and dredge heavily with sugar.

Bake the tart in a preheated oven at 350°F for about 30 minutes, or until the filling is set and the dough is a light golden color. Serve warm or at room temperature.

This tart is a speciality of the northern region of Aosta—my version of a recipe by friend, Carla Tomasi.

caramelized walnut tart

torta di noci valle d'aosta

dough

2⅓ cups all-purpose flour, plus extra for kneading

a pinch of salt

¾ cup sugar

1¾ sticks unsalted butter, cut into cubes and softened

1 whole egg

1 egg yolk

1 teaspoon real vanilla extract

2–3 tablespoons ice water

walnut filling

1¾ cups sugar

½ cup heavy cream, at room temperature

3 cups shelled walnuts, toasted and coarsely chopped

1 egg, beaten, to glaze

sugar, for dusting

wax paper

a tart pan, 10 inches diameter

makes one 10-inch tart
serves 12

To make the dough, sift the flour and salt onto a sheet of wax paper. Put the sugar, butter, whole egg, egg yolk, and vanilla in a food processor and blend until smooth. Add the water and blend again. Pour the flour through the feed tube and pulse until just mixed. Transfer to a lightly floured work surface and knead gently until smooth. Bring together quickly with your hands, knead lightly, and shape into a ball. Wrap in plastic and chill for 30 minutes. If you refrigerate longer than 30 minutes, the dough will become too stiff to roll, so you must return it room temperature for about 20 minutes before rolling.

To make the filling, put the sugar in a heavy saucepan with 6 tablespoons water and melt over gentle heat. When melted, turn up the heat and boil to a pale caramel color, remove from the heat, cool slightly, then stir in the cream and walnuts. Let cool completely.

Unwrap the dough and divide in 2 pieces, one slightly smaller than the other. Roll out the larger piece quite thinly to fit the base and sides of the tart pan. Leave the edges untrimmed and freeze for 15 minutes until hard.

Meanwhile, roll out the smaller piece of dough to make a lid slightly larger than the tart pan. Remove the pan from the freezer, spoon in the walnut filling, then cover with the remaining rolled out dough. Seal the edges, trim, and return to the freezer for 30 minutes until hard. Brush the top with beaten egg and dust with sugar. Make 2 air holes in the dough lid (or prick decoratively all over with a skewer). Bake in a preheated oven at 350°F for 30–40 minutes, until the dough is a rich golden brown. Leave in the pan for 5 minutes, then carefully remove from the pan and transfer to a wire rack to cool.

A real jewel of a tart. The pie crust is filled with a luscious mascarpone and liqueur cream and topped with a sparkling mountain of fresh berries. This looks spectacular, but must be filled at the last moment to prevent the dough from going soggy. Eat with a fork—this one is messy.

fruits of the forest tart

torta ai frutti di bosco

1 recipe Pasta Frolla (page 62)

2 cups mascarpone cheese

1 cup heavy cream

3 tablespoons fruit liqueur or fruit-flavored grappa

1½ lb. fresh mixed berries (strawberries, raspberries, blueberries, wild strawberries, red currants, and/or black currants)

⅓ cup fruit jelly, melted, to glaze

a fluted tart pan with false bottom, 9 inches diameter

serves 6–8
makes one 9-inch tart

Following the method on page 62, make the Pasta Frolla, roll out the dough thinly and use to line the tart pan. Chill or freeze for 15 minutes, bake blind, then cool.

Put the mascarpone, cream, and liqueur in a bowl and beat until thick. Spoon into the tart crust and level the surface. Cover the surface with the berries, mounding them up in the center. Spoon the fruit jelly over the top, then let set in the refrigerator for only 10 minutes before serving or the tart will become soggy.

Variation

Crema Pasticcera
Instead of mascarpone cream, use the traditional custard cream, *Crema Pasticcera* (page 63).

cookies

These crisp little pastries are often made at festival times in all sorts of shapes and sizes. I like to flavor them with exotic cardamom, but you could use grated orange or lemon zest or orange flower water. They can be made a day or two in advance, as long as they are kept in an airtight container. Sprinkle with confectioners' sugar before serving. A rich sherry would do instead of the vin santo or Sicilian Marsala. These are great with ice cream.

cardamom pastry "rags"

cenci al cardamomo

3 cups all-purpose flour, plus extra for rolling

2 large eggs, beaten

⅓ cup light olive oil

½ cup plus 2 tablespoons sugar

10 cardamom pods, seeds removed and crushed

⅓ cup vin santo or Marsala wine

vegetable oil, for frying

confectioners' sugar, for dusting

a deep-fryer

a fluted pastry wheel

serves 12

Sift the flour into a bowl and make a hollow in the center. Pour in the eggs, olive oil, sugar, crushed cardamom seeds, and vin santo.

Mix with a knife, then bring together with your hands and knead into a smooth ball. The dough will be very soft at this point. Wrap in plastic and chill for 1 hour.

Fill a deep-fryer to the recommended level with vegetable oil, then heat to 350°F.

Roll out the dough very thinly on a floured surface. (You may like to do this with half the dough first, then the other half.) Cut into short ribbons with the pastry wheel.

Carefully tie each ribbon into a knot, then deep-fry until palest brown and crisp. Do not over-brown or they will taste bitter. Drain on paper towels. When cold, sprinkle with confectioners' sugar and serve piled up high on a plate.

Delicious, crisp little cookies made with a mixture of freshly ground almonds and pine nuts. If you have any peach or apricot kernels, use these in place of some of the almonds and they will impart a fantastic almond flavor to the cookies—in this case, don't add the almond extract. These are wonderful used as the base for a trifle or served with after-dinner liqueurs.

amaretti cookies with pine nuts

amaretti con pinoli

¾ cup blanched almonds

1 cup pine nuts, plus 3 tablespoons extra, to sprinkle

½ cup sugar

2 extra-large egg whites

1 teaspoon almond extract

a pastry bag fitted with a plain ½-inch tip

2 baking sheets lined with parchment paper

makes about 30

Put the almonds, pine nuts, and 1 tablespoon of the sugar in a food processor fitted with the grater disk. Grind to a fine powder. Alternatively, use a blender or rotary nut grinder. Set aside.

Put the egg whites in a bowl and beat with an electric beater until stiff but not dry. Gradually beat in the remaining sugar until the whites are stiff and shiny. Fold in the ground nuts and almond extract. Spoon the mixture into the pastry bag and pipe it onto the baking sheets in tiny rounds.

Sprinkle with a few extra pine nuts and bake in a preheated oven at 300°F for 30 minutes, until the cookies are lightly browned and hard. Transfer to a wire rack to cool. The cookies may be stored in an airtight container for up to 2 weeks.

Homemade ladyfingers are so much nicer in both texture and taste than the bought variety and have many uses. Children love them, especially for dipping into desserts like zabaglione. They also tend not to become as soggy when soaked in alcohol, as in a *tiramisù*. Make these, and a world of other recipes will open up to you.

ladyfingers

savoiardi

5 eggs, separated

1 teaspoon vanilla extract

½ cup plus 2 tablespoons sugar

a pinch of salt

¾ cup plus 2 tablespoons all-purpose flour

⅓ cup potato flour

confectioners' sugar, for dusting

a pastry bag fitted with a ½-inch plain tip

3 baking sheets lined with nonstick parchment paper

makes about 36 cookies

Put the egg yolks, vanilla, and half the sugar in a bowl and beat for about 5 minutes until pale and fluffy. Put the egg whites in a bowl with a pinch of salt and beat until soft peaks form. Gradually beat in the remaining sugar until stiff and shiny.

Fold the egg white mixture into the yolks. Sift the flour and potato flour over the eggs and fold in carefully. Fill the pastry bag with the mixture. Pipe 4-inch lengths in rows onto the lined baking sheets, spacing them well apart. Sift confectioners' sugar generously over the ladyfingers.

Bake in a preheated oven at 375°F for about 15 minutes until golden and firm to the touch. Remove from the oven and let cool on wire racks.

They keep for 2–3 weeks layered between sheets of parchment paper in an airtight container.

I have always loved the name of these little chocolate and almond cookies from Piedmont in northern Italy. They are delicious and are often made for special occasions, such as christening teas and weddings.

lady's kisses

baci di dama

1½ cups ground almonds, or 2 cups blanched almonds ground in a food processor or blender

a pinch of salt

1¼ sticks unsalted butter, at room temperature

1 cup plus 2 tablespoons sugar

1 teaspoon real vanilla extract

⅔ cup all-purpose flour

2 tablespoons unsweetened cocoa powder

chocolate cream

4 oz. bittersweet chocolate

⅓ cup heavy cream

2 baking sheets, lined with nonstick parchment paper

makes about 24

Put the ground almonds and salt in a bowl and mix well. Put the butter, sugar, and vanilla in a bowl and beat until pale and fluffy. Fold in the ground almonds, sift the flour and cocoa powder over the top, and fold in.

Scoop out teaspoons of mixture and roll into small balls. Arrange the balls spaced well apart on the baking sheets. Press each one to flatten slightly.

Bake in a preheated oven at 350°F for 15 minutes until firm. Remove from the oven, then transfer onto wire racks and let cool.

To make the chocolate cream, put the chocolate and cream in a bowl set over a saucepan of simmering water and heat gently until melted. When melted, remove the bowl from the pan and let cool to room temperature and beginning to thicken. Beat with a hand-held electric beater until cold and thick, then chill until firm.

Bring the chocolate cream to room temperature, then use it to sandwich together 2 cookies at a time. Pile up and serve.

cakes

The word *schiacciata* literally means "flattened." *Schiacciata con uva* is a bread baked with the Chianti grape (Sangiovese) and sugar, and is only seen in baker's shops at grape harvest time. My sweeter, richer version involves red table grapes, walnuts, butter, and brown sugar.

sticky grape and walnut cake

schiacciata all'uva e noci

Put the fresh yeast and sugar in a medium bowl and beat until creamy. Beat in the warm water. Leave for 10 minutes until frothy. For other yeasts, use according to the package instructions.

Sift the flour into a large bowl. Make a hollow in the center. Pour in the yeast mixture, egg yolks, olive oil, and salt. Mix until the dough comes together. Transfer to a lightly floured work surface. Wash and dry your hands and knead for 10 minutes until smooth and elastic. The dough should be quite soft, but if too soft to handle, add more flour. Put in a clean oiled bowl, cover with a damp cloth, and let rise until doubled in size, about 1 hour.

Meanwhile, put the butter, sugar, and lemon zest in a bowl and beat until creamy. Stir in the walnuts and keep at room temperature.

When the dough has risen, punch it down with your fist and cut in half. Shape into 2 balls, flatten and roll out into 2 rounds, 10 inches diameter. Put 1 round in the prepared pan, then spread with half the walnut butter and half the grapes. Put the other round on top and dot with the remaining walnut butter. Press in the remaining grapes and sprinkle with sugar. Cover with a damp cloth and let rise for 1 hour or until puffy and doubled in size.

Uncover the pan and bake in a preheated oven at 400°F for 15 minutes, then reduce the heat to 350°F for another 30 minutes or until well risen and golden brown. Let cool slightly before taking out of the pan. Cut into wedges and serve.

45

Big, sugary, doughnut "bombs" that explode with vanilla custard when you bite them, these are a not-so-delicate delicacy from Tuscany and my favorite breakfast treat.

bomboloni doughnuts

bomboloni con la crema

3⅓ cups all-purpose flour, plus extra for kneading

finely grated zest of 1 unwaxed lemon

a pinch of salt

¾ cup sugar

6 tablespoons unsalted butter, cut into cubes

1⅓ cakes compressed yeast, or one ¼ oz. package active dry yeast

1¼ cups warm milk and water, mixed

½ recipe Crema Pasticcera al Limone (page 63)

vegetable oil, for deep-frying

a plain cookie cutter, 2 inches diameter

a baking sheet, floured

a deep-fat fryer

a pastry bag fitted with a ½-inch plain piping tip

makes about 20 doughnuts

Put the flour, lemon zest, pinch of salt, and half the sugar in a food processor and blend for 1 minute. Add the butter and yeast and blend again until all lumps have disappeared. Pour in the warm milk and water and process until the mixture forms a large ball. Transfer to a floured work surface (the dough should be quite soft, rather than firm—if not, add a little more liquid). Knead the dough for about 10 minutes or until soft and pliable. Transfer to an oiled bowl and put the whole thing inside a plastic bag. Seal and leave in a warm place to rise until doubled in size, 1–2 hours.

Punch down the dough with your fist and knead out any air. Roll out to about ½ inch thick. Using the cookie cutter, stamp out at least 10 rounds, setting them well apart on the floured baking sheet. Put the sheet inside the plastic bag again and let rise until doubled in size.

Fill a deep-fat fryer to the manufacturer's recommended level and heat to 350°F. Fry the risen doughnuts in batches of 2–3 until puffed and golden all over—you will have to flip them over. Drain well on paper towels and toss with some of the remaining sugar. Let cool. When cold, put the crema into a piping bag. Push the tip into a doughnut and squeeze a little crema pasticcera into the center. Alternatively, cut open and fill with the crema, as shown. Set the doughnuts on a serving plate and sprinkle with the remaining sugar.

Note If using active dry yeast, use 1 tablespoon and dissolve it in the warm liquid first. Leave in a warm pace until frothy. Pour this into the flour and butter mixture and mix to form a dough as in the recipe above.

Since first tasting this cake in Tuscany, I make it all the time. It is very light, and studded with juicy chunks of apple. You can change the spice to cinnamon—use more, as it is not as assertive as cloves. Fellow cook Ursula Ferrigno adds finely chopped rosemary to hers, which tastes very special. The whisked sponge method of cake making is popular in Italy.

apple and lemon sponge cake

torta di mele con limone

1 stick unsalted butter

4 well-flavored sweet apples

finely grated zest of 2 unwaxed lemons and the juice of ½ lemon

¼ teaspoon ground cloves

4 large eggs

¾ cup sugar

¾ cup all-purpose flour

1 teaspoon baking powder

a pinch of salt

3 tablespoons apricot jelly, melted, to glaze

a 9-inch springform cake pan or sloping sided moule-á-manque pan, well buttered and base-lined

makes one 9-inch cake serves 8

Melt the butter in a saucepan, then set aside to cool. Peel, core, and cut the apples into medium chunks. Put in a bowl, add the lemon zest, cloves, and juice, and toss to coat.

Put the eggs and sugar in a heatproof bowl and set over a saucepan of simmering water. Using a and hand-held electric beater, whisk for about 15 minutes until glossy, thick, and pale and doubled in volume. The mixture will hold a trail when the beaters are lifted out of the bowl. Remove the bowl from the heat and continue beating for about 5–10 minutes until the mixture is cool.

Sift the flour, baking powder, and salt together into a bowl. Gently fold half the flour into the whisked mixture. Pour the cooled melted butter around the edge of the mixture and fold in. Fold in the remaining flour, then two-thirds of the apples. Be very careful when folding in—you want to keep as much air in the mixture as possible. Spoon the remaining apples into the base of the pan, then pour the cake mixture over the apples. Bake in a preheated oven at 350°F for about 40 minutes until risen, firm in the center, and golden brown.

Remove from the oven and leave in the pan for 5 minutes before inverting onto a wire rack to cool. Brush the apple top with apricot glaze just before serving.

This dark, moist chocolate cake is made all over southern Italy, but particularly in Capri. Normally, it is made using ground almonds, but I have adapted this one to suit those who prefer not to eat nuts—it is equally delicious with a fantastic soft texture. Serve with whipped cream.

dark chocolate cake from capri

torta caprese

7 oz. bittersweet chocolate

2½ sticks unsalted butter, softened

¼ cup espresso coffee

6 eggs, separated

1 cup sugar

scant ⅓ cup potato flour or cornstarch

½ teaspoon baking powder

1 cup stale white bread crumbs

confectioners' sugar, for dusting

whipped cream, to serve

flour, for dusting

a springform cake pan, 10 inches diameter, sides well buttered, bottom lined with nonstick parchment paper

makes one 10-inch cake

Dust the prepared cake pan with flour.

Break up the chocolate and put it in a heatproof bowl. Add the butter. Set over a saucepan of simmering water and stir occasionally until melted. Remove from the heat, stir in the coffee, then cool a little.

Put the egg yolks and half the sugar in a bowl and beat until pale and fluffy. Mix in the potato flour and baking powder. Carefully mix in the chocolate and butter mixture, then fold in the bread crumbs.

Put the egg whites in a bowl, beat until stiff but not dry, then gradually beat in the remaining sugar. Gently fold into the mixture. Pour into the prepared cake pan and bake in a preheated oven at 350°F for about 30 minutes, until risen and almost firm in the center. To test, insert a skewer into the middle of the cake. When removed it should have a little of the mixture clinging to it—this will ensure that the cake is moist. Do not overbake. Invert onto a wire rack to cool, then dust with confectioners' sugar. Serve with whipped cream.

Note To make a smaller cake, halve the quantities and bake in an 8-inch cake pan.

A wonderful fruited and enriched bread with medieval origins. This is not as rich as Milanese panettone, but is delicious and makes fantastic toast.

genoese christmas bread

pandolce

3⅓ cups all-purpose flour, plus extra for kneading

¾ cup sugar

a pinch of salt

4 tablespoons unsalted butter, softened

1 cake compressed yeast, or half a ¼ oz package active dry yeast

½ cup warm milk or water

1 extra-large egg, lightly beaten

2 tablespoons Marsala wine

¼ cup orange flower water

1 tablespoon fennel seeds

1 cup raisins

⅓ cup finely chopped candied peel

½ cup pine nuts

a baking sheet, floured

makes 1 loaf, serves 8

Put the flour, sugar, and a pinch of salt in a food processor and blend for 1 minute. Add the butter and fresh yeast or active dry yeast and blend again until all lumps have disappeared. If using active dry yeast, dissolve it in the warm liquid first. Leave in a warm pace until frothy.

Pour in the warm milk or water (or yeasty milk), egg, Marsala, and orange flower water and process until it forms a large ball. Transfer to a floured work surface (the dough should be quite soft, rather than firm—if not, add a little more warm liquid).

Knead in the fennel seeds, raisins, candied peel, and pine nuts. Transfer to an oiled bowl and put the whole thing inside a plastic bag. Seal and leave in a warm place to rise until puffy—this can take 3–4 hours, because enriched doughs take longer to rise.

Transfer the dough to a floured surface and punch down with your fist. Shape into a small round loaf and put on the floured baking sheet. Cover with a large, upturned bowl and leave in a warm place to rise for 2–3 hours. Use a sharp knife to score 3 slits in the loaf to form a triangle, or 4 slits to form a cross-hatch. Bake in a preheated oven at 375°F for about 1 hour, or until golden brown. Transfer to a wire rack to cool. Wrap well in plastic and it will last for 2 weeks.

candies

cannoliche shells

2 cups all-purpose flour

2 tablespoons unsweetened
cocoa powder

¼ teaspoon ground cinnamon

a pinch of salt

1 tablespoon sugar

about 5 tablespoons sweet white
wine or dry Marsala

2 tablespoons olive oil

1 egg white, lightly beaten

oil, for deep-frying

ricotta filling

1 cup fresh ricotta cheese

½ cup confectioners' sugar, sifted,
plus extra for dusting

2 oz. bittersweet chocolate,
coarsely grated

a pinch of ground cinnamon

2 tablespoons finely chopped
glacé fruits or candied peel
(optional)

a pasta machine or rolling pin

a 3-inch round cookie cutter

*6–8 bamboo canes, cut 3 inches
long, ½-inch diameter (avoiding
the bumps) to make the molds*

a deep-fryer

a pastry bag and tip

makes about 40

The traditional way to shape cannoli is around short lengths of bamboo cane—hence the name *cannoli*, which means "canes." *Cannoliche* are miniature versions made for special occasions or cocktail parties. The filling is rich and sweet—just how it should be—a little goes a long way. They are irresistible.

miniature sicilian cannoli

cannoliche

To make the dough, sift the flour into a bowl with the cocoa, cinnamon, and salt, then stir in the sugar, wine, and olive oil. Knead to form a smooth, workable dough. Wrap in plastic wrap and leave at room temperature to relax for about 1 hour.

To make the filling, push the ricotta through a sieve into a bowl and beat in the confectioners' sugar. Stir in the grated chocolate, cinnamon, and chopped peel. Cover and chill.

Cut the dough into 4 pieces and gradually roll out each piece very thinly with a pasta machine (or by hand if feeling skilful). Using the cookie cutter, stamp out at least 40 rounds from the dough sheets. Lightly roll each round to make an oval shape. Curl each one around a cut cane and brush the overlap with egg white to seal. Don't let the egg white get on the cane or you will never get the cookie off.

Fill a deep-fryer with oil to the manufacturer's recommended level and heat to 375°F. Fry the cannoliche-wrapped canes in batches of 3–4, turning them as they cook. When little bubbles appear all over the dough, the shells are ready. Lift out the cannoliche with a strainer and drain well on paper towels—it helps if you stand them up on their ends. When cool, carefully ease them off the canes.

Fill them with the ricotta mixture using a pastry bag and tip. After filling, dust with confectioners' sugar and serve immediately before they go soggy. Empty shells will keep in an airtight box for 10 days.

The local pasticcera in Menfi, Sicily, makes these little delicacies to order—they are very popular for eating after a long Sunday lunch, or to take as a gift to friends. They are very indulgent.

chocolate choux mushrooms

funghetti di bignè

½ recipe Crema Pasticcera alla Cioccolata (page 63), warmed to room temperature

pasta bignè

¾ cup all-purpose flour

2 tablespoons unsweetened cocoa powder

a pinch of salt

5 tablespoons butter, cut into pieces

3 large eggs, beaten

for dusting

unsweetened cocoa powder

confectioners' sugar

wax paper

a pastry bag, fitted with a ½-inch plain tip

2 baking sheets, lined with nonstick parchment paper

a wire rack

makes about 20

To make the pasta bignè, sift the flour, cocoa powder, and salt together onto a sheet of wax paper. Put the butter and 1 cup water in a heavy saucepan. Bring slowly to a boil so that, by the time the water boils, the butter has completely melted. As soon as the mixture is boiling fast, add the flour mixture and remove the pan from the heat.

Working as fast as you can, beat the mixture hard with a wooden spoon—it will soon become thick and smooth and leave the sides of the pan. Let cool slightly, then beat in the eggs a little at a time, until the mixture is soft, shiny, and smooth. It should be of dropping consistency—not too runny. ("Dropping consistency" means that the mixture will fall off a spoon reluctantly and all in a blob: if it runs off, it is too soft.)

Spoon half the mixture into the pastry bag fitted with the plain tip. Pipe 20 small mounds onto one of the baking sheets, spacing them well apart. Using the remaining mixture, pipe 20 short lengths (about 1 inch) to form the stems of the mushrooms. If there are points of the mixture in the center of the mounds, moisten a fingertip with water and smooth down.

Bake the mushroom tops in a preheated oven at 375°F for about 20 minutes, the stems for 15, until they are well risen and a deep golden color. When cooked, remove from the oven. Make a hole in the tops only, to let the steam escape. Transfer to a wire rack to cool.

Fill the pastry bag with the warmed chocolate crema pasticcera and pipe into the mushroom caps through the hole you have made. Insert a stem into each one. Dust with cocoa and confectioners' sugar and pile onto a dish to serve, or into a gift box.

I have seen versions of this all over Italy, but the best was in a shop in Assisi. It is easy to make and utterly delicious served in slices with coffee. I make it with those lovely bottled wild amarena cherries sold in the pretty blue and white jars. If you can't get them, use dried cherries soaked in a little liqueur.

chocolate, fig, and cherry salami

salame del papa

15 rich tea biscuits or similar

8 oz. bittersweet chocolate, chopped

1½ sticks unsalted butter

3 tablespoons cherry brandy or amarena (wild cherry) syrup

4–6 tablespoons canned amarena cherries, drained, or dried cherries soaked in the warm cherry brandy for 30 minutes

⅔ cup coarsely chopped semi-dried figs

2 sheets edible rice paper (baking, not Asian)

serves 10

Put the tea biscuits in a plastic bag, crush lightly with a rolling pin, then transfer to a large bowl.

Put the chocolate, butter, and cherry brandy in a small saucepan and melt over gentle heat, stirring gently until smooth. Pour the melted chocolate over the crushed biscuits, add the cherries and figs, and mix well. Cover and refrigerate for about 1 hour until the mixture is just beginning to firm up.

Lift the mixture out of the bowl and roll into a long sausage shape. Set the 2 sheets of rice paper on a clean work surface, ends overlapping to make a long rectangle. Wash and dry your hands thoroughly. Put the sausage at the longer edge and roll up to enclose. Cut away any excess and roll gently until the paper sticks well.* Chill for 2–3 hours until firm.

To serve, slice through the paper into thin disks.

*This can be quite tricky, so if your patience runs out, roll up the sausage in nonstick parchment paper, chill until firm, then roll in confectioners' sugar and slice thinly.

This divinely chewy after-dinner sweetmeat looks lovely wrapped in colored waxed papers and is served everywhere in Italy at Christmas time.

italian nougat

torrone

6–8 sheets edible rice paper (baking, not Asian), for lining

⅔ cup blanched almonds

1⅛ cups whole hazelnuts

⅔ cup skinned pistachios

¾ cup clear honey (I like acacia blossom)

2 extra-large egg whites (¼ cup plus 2 teaspoons)

2 teaspoons vanilla extract

1 cup sugar

3 tablespoons light corn syrup

2 baking pans, 6½ x 1 inch

2 baking pans, 10 x 6½ x 1 inch or 1 Swiss roll tin, 16 x 10 x 1 inch

2 baking sheets

a candy thermometer

makes about 1½ lb.

Line the bottom of the baking pans with the rice paper. Spread the almonds and hazelnuts on separate baking sheets and toast in a preheated oven at 400°F for 5–8 minutes until golden. Remove from the oven. Let the almonds cool on a plate. Put the hazelnuts in a clean cloth and rub off the skins.

Put the honey in a wide saucepan and melt over low heat. Drop in a candy thermometer, bring to a boil, and boil steadily until the honey reaches the soft-ball stage, 240°F.

While the honey is cooking, beat the egg whites in a food mixer until firm peaks form. They should be ready at the same time as the honey, not before. When the honey is ready, pour it over the egg whites, with the machine still running. Continue beating for 5–8 minutes until thick and cooled. Beat in the vanilla.

Put the sugar, syrup, and 2 tablespoons water in a wide saucepan and melt over low heat. When dissolved, drop in a candy thermometer and bring to a boil. Boil steadily until the syrup reaches the hard-crack stage (285°F). Remove from the heat and, just when it has stopped bubbling, pour onto the egg-white-and-honey mixture, beating all the while (in the machine) until the mixture is really thick and glossy. Remove the mixture from the machine and stir in the nuts. Spoon the torrone carefully into the rice-paper-lined pans in blobs, then spread flat—it should be about ½ inch thick. Cover with more rice paper, then lift one pan on top of the other and press down gently to level the surface. Repeat, but vice-versa.

Let cool to room temperature, then cut into squares, bars, or long slices. When completely cold, wrap well in plastic and store in an airtight container in a cool place for up to 1 week.

This rich, crumbly dough with a cookie-like texture is used to make most Italian pastry *dolci.* This is the easy, food processor method, that keeps the dough cool. As always, don't overwork the dough, as this can toughen it.

italian tart crust dough

pasta frolla

1⅔ cups all-purpose flour, plus extra for kneading

a pinch of salt

6 tablespoons sugar

1 stick unsalted butter, cut into pieces

2 large eggs, lightly beaten

I teaspoon vanilla extract

2 tablespoons ice water

wax paper

a tart pan, 9 inches diameter

foil or all-purpose plastic wrap and baking beans

a baking sheet

makes one 9-inch pie crust

Sift the flour and salt onto a sheet of wax paper. Put the sugar, butter, eggs, and vanilla extract in a food processor and blend until smooth. Add the water and blend again.

Pour the flour through the tube and work until just mixed. Invert onto a lightly floured work surface and knead gently until smooth. Bring together quickly with your hands, knead lightly, shape into a ball, then flatten to a round cake. Wrap in plastic and chill for 30 minutes. If you refrigerate longer than 30 minutes, the dough will become too stiff to roll, so leave it at room temperature for about 20 minutes before rolling. Unwrap the dough and put on a well-floured work surface. Roll to about ¼ inch thick, then use to line the tart pan. Prick the base all over with a fork, then chill or freeze for 15 minutes to set the dough.

Line with foil or all-purpose plastic wrap (flicking the edges in towards the center so it doesn't catch on the dough). Fill with baking beans, set on a baking sheet, and bake in the center of a preheated oven at 375°F for 10–12 minutes for open tarts, 4–5 for tartlets. Remove the foil or plastic and beans and return the tart crust(s) to the oven for a further 5–7 (2–3) minutes to dry out completely.

Tip To prevent a tart crust from becoming soggy from the filling (especially egg and cream fillings), brush the blind-baked crust (hot or cold) with beaten egg and bake again for 2–4 minutes until set and shiny. This will also fill and seal any holes made when pricking the dough before baking blind. If necessary, repeat the process to build up an impervious layer.

italian pastry cream or custard

crema pasticcera

2 cups whole milk

½ cup sugar

6 extra-large egg yolks

a pinch of salt

¼ cup all-purpose flour

2 teaspoons real vanilla extract

makes about 2½ cups

Put the milk and half the sugar in a medium saucepan and heat to just below boiling point.

Put the egg yolks, salt, and remaining sugar in a bowl and beat until pale and fluffy. Sift in the flour and beat in.

Remove the milk from the heat and gradually beat it into the egg mixture. Pour the mixture back into the saucepan, return to the heat and beat constantly until the cream thickens and comes to a boil. Continue boiling and beating for 30 seconds to cook the flour.

Remove from the heat, beat in the vanilla, then pour into a bowl. Press plastic wrap over the surface and refrigerate until cold—this will prevent a skin forming. Use the cream within 24 hours.

Variations

Crema Pasticcera al Limone Add the finely grated zest of 1 unwaxed lemon to the milk and sugar while heating.

Crema Pasticcera alla Cioccolata Add 4 oz. grated bittersweet chocolate to the cooked crema and stir until dissolved. Cover and chill as above.

index

conversion charts

Weights and measures have been rounded up or down slightly to make measuring easier.

Volume equivalents:

American	Metric	Imperial
1 teaspoon	5 ml	
1 tablespoon	15 ml	
¼ cup	60 ml	2 fl.oz.
⅓ cup	75 ml	2½ fl.oz.
½ cup	125 ml	4 fl.oz.
⅔ cup	150 ml	5 fl.oz. (¼ pint)
¾ cup	175 ml	6 fl.oz.
1 cup	250 ml	8 fl.oz.

Weight equivalents: **Measurements:**

Imperial	Metric	Inches	Cm
1 oz.	25 g	¼ inch	5 mm
2 oz.	50 g	½ inch	1 cm
3 oz.	75 g	¾ inch	1.5 cm
4 oz.	125 g	1 inch	2.5 cm
5 oz.	150 g	2 inches	5 cm
6 oz.	175 g	3 inches	7 cm
7 oz.	200 g	4 inches	10 cm
8 oz. (½ lb.)	250 g	5 inches	12 cm
9 oz.	275 g	6 inches	15 cm
10 oz.	300 g	7 inches	18 cm
11 oz.	325 g	8 inches	20 cm
12 oz.	375 g	9 inches	23 cm
13 oz.	400 g	10 inches	25 cm
14 oz.	425 g	11 inches	28 cm
15 oz.	475 g	12 inches	30 cm
16 oz. (1 lb.)	500 g		
2 lb.	1 kg		

Oven temperatures:

110°C	(225°F)	Gas ¼
120°C	(250°F)	Gas ½
140°C	(275°F)	Gas 1
150°C	(300°F)	Gas 2
160°C	(325°F)	Gas 3
180°C	(350°F)	Gas 4
190°C	(375°F)	Gas 5
200°C	(400°F)	Gas 6
220°C	(425°F)	Gas 7
230°C	(450°F)	Gas 8
240°C	(475°F)	Gas 9